By

Rev. Thomas J. Donaghy

C.B.   P.C.

CATHOLIC BOOK PUBLISHING CORP.
New Jersey

NIHIL OBSTAT: Rev. Msgr. James M. Cafone, M.A., S.T.D.
Censor Librorum
IMPRIMATUR: ✠ Most Rev. John J. Myers, J.C.D., D.D.
Archbishop of Newark

(T-38)

ISBN 978-0-89942-076-9

20 WW 1

CONTENTS

THE MASS—OUR GREATEST PRAYER

Essence of the Mass

AT the Last Supper, our Savior instituted the Eucharistic sacrifice of His Body and Blood. He did this in order to perpetuate the sacrifice of the Cross throughout the centuries until He should come again.

Each year through the Liturgy (especially Mass), the Church makes present for us the Life, Death, and Resurrection of Jesus. In this way, we can encounter our Lord in His Mysteries, give glory to God, and obtain graces for ourselves and the whole world.

Thus, the Mass is the greatest prayer we have. Through it we give thanks and praise to the Father for the wonderful future He has given us in His Son. We also ask forgiveness for our sins and beg the Father's blessing upon us and all human beings.

Major Parts of Holy Mass

Introductory Rites—*We speak to God in acts of contrition, praise, and petition.*

Liturgy of the Word—*We listen to what God says to us in the Readings, the Gospel, and the Homily.*

Liturgy of the Eucharist—

Preparation of the Gifts—*With the priest we present the gifts of bread and wine.*

Eucharistic Prayer—*At the consecration this bread and wine are changed into the Body and Blood of Jesus.*

Communion Rite—*We receive Jesus, Who gives of Himself selflessly in love.*

Concluding Rites—*We receive God's blessing and go forth to bring the good news of Jesus to others by word and example.*

DAILY PRAYERS

The Sign of the Cross

IN the name of the Father, and of the Son, ✠ and of the Holy Spirit. Amen.

The Apostles' Creed

I BELIEVE in God, the Father Almighty, Creator of heaven and earth, and in Jesus Christ, His only Son, Our Lord, Who was conceived by the Holy Spirit, born of the Virgin Mary, suffered under Pontius Pilate, was crucified, died, and was buried; He descended into hell; on the third day He rose again from the dead; He ascended into heaven, and is seated at the right hand of God the Father Almighty; from there He will come to judge the living and the dead.

I believe in the Holy Spirit, the holy catholic Church, the communion of saints, the forgiveness of sins, the resurrection of the body, and life everlasting. Amen.

The Lord's Prayer

OUR Father Who art in heaven, hallowed be Thy name; Thy kingdom come, Thy will be done on earth as it is in heaven. Give us this day our daily bread, and forgive us our trespasses, as we forgive those who trespass against us; and lead us not into temptation, but deliver us from evil. Amen.

The Hail Mary

HAIL, Mary, full of grace! The Lord is with thee; blessed art thou among women, and blessed is the fruit of thy womb, Jesus. Holy Mary, Mother of God, pray for us sinners now and at the hour of our death. Amen.

Glory Be to the Father

GLORY be to the Father, and to the Son, and to the Holy Spirit. As it was in the beginning, is now, and ever shall be. Amen.

How to Say the Rosary

1. Begin on the crucifix and say the Apostles' Creed.
2. On the 1st bead, say 1 Our Father.
3. On the next 3 beads, say a Hail Mary.
4. Next say 1 Glory Be. Then announce and think of the first Mystery and what it means, and say 1 Our Father.
5. Say 10 Hail Marys and 1 Glory be to the Father.
6. Announce the second Mystery and continue in the same way until each of the five Mysteries of the selected group or decade is said.

The Joyful Mysteries

Said on Mondays and Saturdays [except during Lent], and the Sundays from Advent to Lent

1. The Angel Gabriel brings the joyful message to Mary.
2. Mary visits her cousin Elizabeth.
3. Jesus is born in a stable in Bethlehem.
4. Jesus is presented in the Temple.
5. Jesus is found in the Temple.

The Luminous Mysteries

Said on Thursdays [except during Lent]

1. Jesus is baptized in the Jordan.
2. Jesus reveals Himself at Cana.
3. Jesus proclaims God's Kingdom.
4. Jesus is transfigured.
5. Jesus institutes the Eucharist.

The Sorrowful Mysteries

Said on Tuesdays and Fridays throughout the year, and every day from Ash Wednesday until Easter

1. Jesus prays in agony to His Heavenly Father.
2. Jesus is scourged.
3. Jesus is crowned with thorns.
4. Jesus carries His Cross to Calvary.
5. Jesus dies on the Cross.

The Glorious Mysteries

Said on Wednesdays [except during Lent], and Sundays from Easter to Advent

1. Jesus rises from death.
2. Jesus ascends to Heaven.

3. The Holy Spirit descends upon the Apostles.
4. Mary is taken up to Heaven in body and soul.
5. Mary is crowned in Heaven.

Prayer to the Holy Spirit

COME, Holy Spirit, fill the hearts of Your faithful and kindle in them the fire of Your love.

℣. Send forth Your Spirit, and they shall be created.

℞. And You shall renew the face of the earth.

Let us pray. O God, You instructed the hearts of the faithful by the light of the Holy Spirit. Grant that, by the gift of the same Spirit, we may be always truly wise, and ever rejoice in His consolation. Through Christ our Lord. Amen.

Hail, Holy Queen

HAIL, Holy Queen, Mother of mercy, hail, our life, our sweetness, and our hope! To you do we cry, poor banished children of Eve! To you do we send up our sighs, mourning, and weeping in this vale of tears!

Turn then, most gracious advocate, your eyes of mercy toward us; and after this, our exile, show unto us the blessed fruit of your womb, Jesus! O clement, O loving, O sweet Virgin Mary!

Morning Offering

O JESUS, through the Immaculate Heart of Mary, I offer You my prayers, works, joys and sufferings of this day for all the intentions of Your Sacred Heart, in union with the Holy Sacrifice of the Mass throughout the world, in reparation for my sins, for the intentions of all our associates, and in particular for all the intentions of this month *(mention intention if known).*

Act of Spiritual Communion

M Y Jesus, I believe that You are in the Blessed Sacrament. I love You above all things, and I long for You in my soul. Since I cannot now receive You sacramentally, come at least spiritually into my heart.

I know You have already come. I embrace You and unite myself entirely to You; never permit me to be separated from You.

Blessing before Meals

BLESS us, O Lord, and these Your gifts, which we are about to receive from Your bounty, through Christ our Lord. Amen.

Grace after Meals

WE give You thanks for all Your benefits, O Almighty God, Who live and reign forever. Amen.

May the souls of the faithful departed, through the mercy of God, rest in peace. Amen.

Evening Prayer

O MY God, I adore You, and I love You with all my heart. I thank You for having created me, having saved me by Your grace, and for having preserved me during this day. I pray that You will take for Yourself whatever good I might have done this day, and that You will forgive me whatever evil I might have done. Protect me this night, and may Your grace be with me always and with those I love.

Act of Faith

O MY God, I firmly believe that You are one God in three Divine Persons, Father, Son, and Holy Spirit. I believe that Your Divine Son became Man, and died for our sins, and He will come to judge the living and the dead.

I believe these and all the truths that the Holy Catholic Church teaches because You have revealed them, Who can neither deceive nor be deceived.

Act of Hope

O MY God, relying on Your almighty power and infinite mercy and promises, I hope to obtain pardon for my sins, the help of Your grace, and life everlasting, through the merits of Jesus Christ, my Lord and Redeemer.

Act of Love

O MY God, I love You above all things, with my whole heart and soul, because You are all-good and worthy of all love.

I love my neighbor as myself for the love of You. I forgive all who have injured me, and ask pardon of all whom I have injured.

Act of Contrition

O MY God, I am heartily sorry for having offended You, and I detest all my sins because of Your just punishments, but most of all because they offend You, my God, Who are all-good and deserving of all my love. I firmly resolve, with the help of Your grace, to sin no more and to avoid the near occasions of sin. Amen.

The Angelus

℣. The Angel of the Lord declared unto Mary.

℟. And she conceived of the Holy Spirit.

Hail Mary, etc.

℣. Behold the handmaid of the Lord.

℟. Be it done unto me according to your word.

Hail Mary, etc.

℣. And the Word was made flesh.

℟. And dwelt among us.

Hail Mary, etc.

℣. Pray for us, O holy Mother of God.

℟. That we may be made worthy of the promises of Christ.

Let us pray. Pour forth, we beseech You, O Lord, Your grace into our hearts, that we to whom the Incarnation of Christ, Your Son, was made known by the message of an Angel, may by His

Passion and Cross be brought to the glory of His Resurrection, through the same Christ our Lord. Amen.

Regina Caeli

(Said during Eastertide instead of Angelus)

QUEEN of heaven, rejoice, alleluia. For He Whom you merited to bear, alleluia.
Has risen as He said, alleluia.
Pray for us to God, alleluia.

℣. Rejoice and be glad, O Virgin Mary, alleluia.
℟. Because the Lord is truly risen, alleluia.

Let us pray. O God, by the Resurrection of Your Son, our Lord Jesus Christ, You granted joy to the whole world. Grant, we beg You, that, through the intercession of the Virgin Mary, His Mother, we may attain the joys of eter-

nal life. Through the same Christ our
Lord. Amen.

Prayers to My Guardian Angel

ANGEL of God, my guardian dear, to
whom His love entrusts me here,
ever this night be at my side, to light
and guard, to rule and guide. Amen.

DEAR Angel, in His goodness God
gave you to me to guide, protect,
and enlighten me, and to bring me
back to the right way when I go astray.

Encourage me when I am disheartened, and instruct me when I err in my
judgment. Help me to become more
Christlike, and so some day to be
accepted into the company of Angels
and Saints in heaven.

Serenity Prayer

GOD, grant me the serenity
To accept the things
I cannot change . . .
Courage to change the things I can . . .
And wisdom to know the difference.

Anima Christi

SOUL of Christ, sanctify me.
Body of Christ, save me.
Blood of Christ, inebriate me.
Water from the side of Christ, wash me.
Passion of Christ, strengthen me.
O good Jesus, hear me.
Within Your wounds, hide me.
Separated from You let me never be.
From the malignant enemy, defend me.
At the hour of my death, call me.
To come to You, bid me,
That I may praise You in the company
Of Your Saints, for all eternity. Amen.

The "Memorare"

REMEMBER, O most gracious Virgin Mary, that never was it known that anyone who fled to your protection, implored your help or sought your intercession was left unaided. Inspired with this confidence, I fly to you, O Virgin of virgins, my Mother; to you do I come, before you I stand, sinful and sorrowful. O Mother of the Word Incarnate, despise not my petitions, but in your mercy hear and answer me. Amen.

Canticle of Mary

MY SOUL proclaims the greatness of the Lord; my spirit finds its joy in God my Savior. For He has looked upon His handmaid in her lowliness; all future generations shall call me blessed. God Who is all-powerful has done wondrous deeds for me, and blessed is His Name. His mercy has been shown throughout every age to those who fear Him.

The Lord has shown great power with His arm; He has bewildered the proud in their inmost thoughts. He has unseated the mighty from their thrones and raised up the lowly. The hungry He has provided with every choice food while the rich He has sent away unfed. He has given unfailing support to Israel His servant, always mindful of His mercy, as He promised our fathers, promised Abraham and His descendants forever.

PRAYERS TO THE SAINTS

St. Joseph

DEAR St. Joseph, you are an outstanding model of one who strove for holiness every day of your life on earth. Obtain for us the grace to strive for Christian perfection in all that we do or say. Help us to keep the Commandments of God and of His Holy Church and to practice the Evangelical Counsels in the way that applies to our state in life.

Give us such an awareness of God's mercies that with truly thankful hearts we may show forth His praise, not only with our lips, but also in our lives. Let us give ourselves to His service and walk before Him in holiness and righteousness all our days.

May we then attain to that holiness which you and Mary now enjoy with all the Saints in the presence of the Blessed Trinity.

Prayer to St. Michael the Archangel

ST. Michael the Archangel, defend us in the day of battle; be our safeguard against the wiles and wickedness of the devil.

May God rebuke him, we humbly pray, and do thou, O prince of the heavenly host, by the power of God cast into hell Satan and all the other evil spirits, who prowl through the world, seeking the ruin of souls.

Prayer to St. Monica

Patroness of Mothers

EXEMPLARY Mother of the great Augustine, you perseveringly pursued your wayward son with love and affection and pardon and counsel and powerful cries to heaven.

Intercede for all mothers in our day so that they may learn to draw their children to God. Teach them how to remain close to their children, even the prodigal sons and daughters who have sadly gone astray.

Prayer to St. Therese of the Child Jesus

Patroness of Missionaries

DEAR Little Flower of Lisieux, how wonderful was the short life you led. Though cloistered, you went far and wide through fervent prayers and great sufferings. You obtained from God untold helps and graces for His evangelists.

Help all missionaries and teach all of us to spread Christianity in our own neighborhoods and family circles.

Prayer to St. Jude

ST. Jude, apostle of Christ, the Church honors and prays to you universally as the patron of hopeless and difficult cases.

Pray for us in our needs. Make use, we implore you, of this powerful privilege given to you to bring visible and speedy help where it is needed. Pray that we humbly accept the trials and disappointments and mistakes that are a part of our human nature.

Let us see the reflection of the sufferings of Christ in our daily trials and tribulations. Let us see in a spirit of great faith and hope the part we even now share in the joy of Christ's Resurrection, and which we long to share fully in heaven. Intercede that we may again experience this joy in answer to our present needs if it is God's desire for us. *(Here make your request.)*

Prayer to St. Peregrine

Patron of Cancer Patients

O GREAT St. Peregrine, obtain for me the strength to accept my trials from the loving hand of God with patience and resignation. May suffering lead me to a better life and enable me to atone for my own sins and the sins of the world.

St. Peregrine, help me to imitate you in bearing whatever cross God may permit to come to me. Uniting myself with Jesus Crucified and the Mother of Sorrows, I offer my sufferings to God with all the love of my heart, for His glory and the salvation of souls, especially my own. Amen.

St. Pio of Pietrelcina

H UMBLE St. Pio of Pietrelcina, who loved the Catholic Church and served it so well, pray for us. Through your intercession may God send us priests, religious brothers and sisters and dedicated lay ministers to do your work.

Devoted St. Pio of Pietrelcina, who had a great love for the souls in purgatory and offered your own suffering for their release, let us continue your work through our prayers and sacrifices so that they may gain eternal life with you.

Virtuous St. Pio of Pietrelcina, you loved Mary, our Mother and were rewarded with her powerful consolations to endure hardship and suffering. Help us to be attentive to Mary, so that she may intercede for the needs of the world.

O great St. Pio of Pietrelcina, you bore the signs of the Passion of Our Lord Jesus Christ on your body, enduring great suffering in body, mind and spirit. We implore you to strengthen our resolve as we face the pain and suffering of our lives and offer them for the glory of God and for our eternal reward in Heaven.

PRAYERS OF THE SAINTS

St. Francis of Assisi

LORD make me an instrument of your peace. Where there is hatred, let me sow love; where there is injury, pardon; where there is friction, union; where there is error, truth; where there is doubt, faith; where there is despair, hope; where there is darkness, light; and where there is sadness, joy.

O Divine Master, grant that I may not so much seek to be consoled as to console, to be understood as to understand, to be loved as to love.

For it is in giving that we receive, it is in pardoning that we are pardoned, and it is in dying that we are born to eternal life.

St. Augustine

MY brothers and sisters, let us be wary of praying to Christ with our mouths but remaining mute in our life. Who is it that prays to Christ? The person who spurns worldly pleasures. The person who says—not in words but in conduct—"The world had been crucified to me and I to the world" (Gal 6:14). The person who lavishly gives to the poor. (Ps 112:9).

Rest assured, my brothers and sisters, you will receive. Ask, seek, knock; you will receive and find, and it will be opened to you. However, do not ask, seek, and knock with your voice alone but with your life as well. Do the works your life should never be without.

Serm. 88; Serm. Morin 16, 8

St. Ignatius

For Generosity

LORD Jesus, teach me to be gener-
ous; teach me to serve You as You
deserve, to give and not to count the
cost, to fight and not to heed the wounds,
to toil and not to seek for rest, to labor
and not to seek reward, except that of
knowing that I do Your will. Amen.

Prayer of Self-Offering To God

TAKE, O Lord,
and receive my entire liberty,
my memory, my understanding, and my
        whole will.
All that I am and all that I possess
You have given me.
I surrender it all to You
to be disposed of according to Your Will.
Give me only Your love and Your grace;
with these I will be rich enough
and will desire nothing more.

St. Patrick

CHRIST, be with me, Christ before
me,
Christ behind me,

Christ in me, Christ beneath me,
  Christ above me,

Christ on my right, Christ on my left,

Christ where I lie, Christ where I sit,
  Christ where I arise,

Christ in the heart of everyone
  who thinks of me,

Christ in the mouth of everyone
  who speaks of me,

Christ in every eye that sees me,

Christ in every ear that hears me.
  Salvation is of the Lord.
  Salvation is of the Lord.
  Salvation is of the Christ.

May Your salvation, O Lord, be ever
  with us.

FAVORITE PSALMS

Psalm 23

THE LORD is my shepherd;
   there is nothing I shall lack.
He makes me lie down in green pastures;
      He leads me to tranquil streams.
He restores my soul,
         guiding me in paths of righteous-
            ness
      so that His name may be glorified.
Even though I wander
      through the valley of the shadow of
         death,
I will fear no evil,
      for You are at my side,
with Your rod and Your staff
      that comfort me.

You spread a table for me
      in the presence of my enemies.
You anoint my head with oil;
      my cup overflows.
Only goodness and kindness will follow
      me
      all the days of my life,

and I will dwell in the house of the LORD
  forever and ever.

Psalm 27

THE LORD is my light and my salvation;
  whom should I fear?
The LORD is the stronghold of my life;
  of whom should I be afraid?

When evildoers close in on me
  to devour my flesh,
it is they, my adversaries and enemies,
  who stumble and fall.

Even if an army encamps against me,
  my heart will not succumb to fear;
even if war breaks out against me,
  I will not have my trust shaken.

There is only one thing I ask of the
  LORD,
  just one thing I seek:
to dwell in the house of the LORD
  all the days of my life,

so that I may enjoy the beauty of the
    LORD
    and gaze on His temple.
For He will hide me in His shelter
    in times of trouble.
He will conceal me under the cover of
    His tent
    and place me high upon a rock.

I am confident that I will behold the
    goodness of the LORD
    in the land of the living.
Place your hope in the LORD:
    be strong and courageous in your
    heart,
    and place your hope in the LORD.

Psalm 51

HAVE mercy on me, O God,
    in accord with Your kindness;
in Your abundant compassion
    wipe away my offenses.
Wash me completely from my guilt,
    and cleanse me from my sin.

For I am fully aware of my offense,
    and my sin is ever before me.
Against You, You alone, have I sinned;
    I have done what is evil in Your sight.

Therefore, You are right in accusing me
    and just in passing judgment.
Indeed, I was born in iniquity,
        and in sin did my mother conceive
        me.

But You desire sincerity of heart;
    and You endow my innermost being
        with wisdom.
Sprinkle me with hyssop so that I may
        be cleansed;
    wash me until I am whiter than snow.

Let me experience joy and gladness;
    let the bones You have crushed exult.
Hide Your face from my sins,
    and wipe out all my offenses.

Create in me a clean heart, O God,
    and renew a resolute spirit within me.
Do not cast me out from Your presence

or take away from me Your Holy
  Spirit.

Restore to me the joy of being saved,
  and grant me the strength of a gener-
    ous spirit.
I will teach Your ways to the wicked,
  and sinners will return to You.

Deliver me from bloodguilt, O God,
      the God of my salvation,
    and I will proclaim Your righteous-
      ness.
O Lord, open my lips,
  and my mouth will proclaim Your
    praise.

For You take no delight in sacrifice;
  if I were to make a burnt offering,
  You would refuse to accept it.
My sacrifice, O God, is a broken spirit;
  a contrite and humble heart, O God,
  You will not spurn.

Psalm 42

AS a deer longs for running streams,
  so my soul longs for You, O God.
My soul thirsts for God, the living God.
  When shall I come to behold the face
    of God?

My tears have become my food
  day and night,
while people taunt me all day long, say-
    ing,
  "Where is your God?"
As I pour out my soul,
  I recall those times
when I journeyed with the multitude
    and led them in procession to the
      house of God,
amid loud cries of joy and thanksgiving
    on the part of the crowd keeping fes-
      tival.

Why are you so disheartened, O my
    soul?
  Why do you sigh within me?

Place your hope in God,
  for I will once again praise Him,
  my Savior and my God.

Psalm 67

O GOD, be gracious to us and bless
  us
  and let Your face shine upon us.
Then Your ways will be known on earth
  and Your salvation among all nations.
Let the peoples praise You, O God;
  let all the peoples praise You.

Let the nations rejoice and exult,
  for You judge the peoples fairly
  and guide the nations upon the earth.
Let the peoples praise You, O God;
  let all the peoples praise You.

The earth has yielded its harvest;
  God, our God, has blessed us.
May God continue to bless us
  and be revered to the ends of the
  earth.

LITANIES

Litany of the Blessed Virgin Mary

L ORD, have mercy.
Christ, have mercy.
Lord, have mercy,
Christ, hear us.
Christ, graciously hear us.
God, the Father of heaven, *have mercy on us.*
God, the Son, Redeemer of the world, *have mercy on us.*
God, the Holy Spirit, *have mercy on us.*
Holy Trinity, one God, *have mercy on us.*
Holy Mary,
   —*Pray for us.* *
Holy Mother of God,
Holy Virgin of virgins,
Mother of Christ,
Mother of the Church,
Mother, of divine grace,
Mother most pure,

*(After each invocation, respond with *"Pray for us."*)

Mother most chaste,
Mother inviolate,
Mother undefiled,
Mother most amiable,
Mother most admirable,
Mother of good counsel,
Mother of our Creator,
Mother of our Savior,
Virgin most prudent,
Virgin most venerable,
Virgin most renowned,
Virgin most powerful,
Virgin most merciful,
Virgin most faithful,
Mirror of justice,
Seat of wisdom,
Cause of our joy,
Spiritual vessel,
Vessel of honor,
Singular vessel of devotion,
Mystical Rose,
Tower of David,
Tower of ivory,

House of gold,
Ark of the covenant,
Gate of heaven,
Morning star,
Health of the sick,
Refuge of sinners,
Comfort of the afflicted,
Help of Christians,
Queen of angels,
Queen of patriarchs,
Queen of prophets,
Queen of apostles,
Queen of martyrs,
Queen of confessors,
Queen of virgins,
Queen of all saints,
Queen conceived without original sin,
Queen assumed into heaven,
Queen of the most holy Rosary,
Queen of families,
Queen of peace,

Lamb of God, You take away the sins of the world; *spare us, O Lord.*

Lamb of God, You take away the sins of the world; *graciously hear us, O Lord.*

Lamb of God, You take away the sins of the world; *have mercy on us.*

℣. Pray for us, O holy Mother of God,

℟. *That we may be made worthy of the promises of Christ.*

L ET us pray. Grant, we beg You, O Lord God, that we Your servants may enjoy lasting health of mind and body, and by the glorious intercession of the Blessed Mary, ever Virgin, be delivered from present sorrow and enter into the joy of eternal happiness. Through Christ our Lord.

℟. *Amen.*

Litany of St. Joseph

LORD, have mercy.
Christ, have mercy.

Lord, have mercy,

Christ, hear us.
Christ, graciously hear us.

God, the Father of heaven, *have mercy on us.*

God, the Son, Redeemer of the world, *have mercy on us.*

God, the Holy Spirit, *have mercy on us.*

Holy Trinity, one God, *have mercy on us.*

Holy Mary,
   —*Pray for us.**

St. Joseph,

Renowned offspring of David,

Light of patriarchs,

Spouse of the Mother of God,

Chaste guardian of the Virgin,

*(After each invocation, respond with *"Pray for us."*)

Foster-father of the Son of God,
Diligent protector of Christ,
Head of the Holy Family,
Joseph, most just,
Joseph, most chaste,
Joseph, most prudent,
Joseph, most strong,
Joseph, most obedient,
Joseph, most faithful,
Mirror of patience,
Lover of poverty,
Model of artisans,
Glory of home life,
Guardian of virgins,
Pillar of families,
Solace of the wretched,
Hope of the sick,
Patron of the dying,
Terror of demons,
Protector of Holy Church,

Lamb of God, You take away the sins
    of the world; *spare us, O Lord!*

Lamb of God, You take away the sins of the world; *graciously hear us, O Lord!*

Lamb of God, You take away the sins of the world; *have mercy on us.*

℣. He made him the lord of His household,

℟. *And prince over all His possessions.*

LET us pray, O God, in Your ineffable Providence You were pleased to choose Blessed Joseph to be the spouse of Your most holy Mother; grant, we beg You, that we may be worthy to have him for our intercessor in heaven whom on earth we venerate as our Protector: You Who live and reign forever and ever.

℟. *Amen.*

Litany of the Sacred Heart of Jesus

L ORD, have mercy.
Christ, have mercy.

Lord, have mercy,

Christ, hear us.

Christ, graciously hear us.

God, the Father of heaven, *have mercy on us.*

God, the Son, Redeemer of the world, *have mercy on us.**

God, the Holy Spirit,

Holy Trinity, one God,

Heart of Jesus, Son of the eternal Father,

Heart of Jesus, formed by the Holy Spirit in the womb of the Virgin Mother,

Heart of Jesus, substantially united to the Word of God,

Heart of Jesus, of infinite majesty,

Heart of Jesus, sacred temple of God,

*(After each invocation, respond with *"Have mercy on us."*)

Heart of Jesus, tabernacle of the Most High,

Heart of Jesus, house of God and gate of heaven,

Heart of Jesus, burning furnace of charity,

Heart of Jesus, abode of justice and love,

Heart of Jesus, full of goodness and love,

Heart of Jesus, abyss of all virtues,

Heart of Jesus, most worthy of all praise,

Heart of Jesus, King and center of all hearts,

Heart of Jesus, in Whom are all the treasures of wisdom and knowledge,

Heart of Jesus, in Whom dwells the fullness of Divinity,

Heart of Jesus, in Whom the Father was well pleased,

Heart of Jesus, of Whose fullness we have all received,

Heart of Jesus, desire of the everlasting hills,

Heart of Jesus, patient and most merciful,

Heart of Jesus, enriching all who invoke You,

Heart of Jesus, fountain of life and holiness,

Heart of Jesus, propitiation for our sins,

Heart of Jesus, loaded down with opprobrium,

Heart of Jesus, bruised for our offenses,

Heart of Jesus, obedient to death,

Heart of Jesus, pierced with a lance,

Heart of Jesus, source of all consolation,

Heart of Jesus, our life and resurrection,

Heart of Jesus, our peace and reconciliation,

Heart of Jesus, victim for our sins,

Heart of Jesus, salvation of those who trust in You,

Heart of Jesus, hope of those who die in You,

Heart of Jesus, delight of all the Saints,

Lamb of God, You take away the sins of the world; *spare us, O Lord!*

Lamb of God, You take away the sins of the world; *graciously hear us, O Lord!*

Lamb of God, You take away the sins of the world; *have mercy on us.*

℣. Jesus, meek and humble of Heart,

℟. *Make our hearts like to Yours.*

LET us pray, Almighty and eternal God, look upon the Heart of Your most beloved Son and upon the praises and satisfaction that He offers You in the name of sinners; and to those who implore Your mercy, in Your great goodness, grant forgiveness in the Name of the same Jesus Christ, Your Son, Who lives and reigns with You forever and ever.

℟. *Amen.*

Stations of the Cross

1. JESUS IS CONDEMNED TO DEATH
Jn 3:16; Is 53:7; 15:13

Jesus, teach me to appreciate Your sanctifying grace more and more. Help me never to lose it by sin.

2. JESUS BEARS HIS CROSS
Is 53:4; Lk 9:23; Mk 11:28f

Lord Jesus, may I love You always and bear my crosses for Your sake.

3. JESUS FALLS THE FIRST TIME
Lam 3:16f; Is 53:6; Jn 1:29

Jesus, make me strong enough to conquer all my wicked passions.

4. JESUS MEETS HIS MOTHER
Lk 2:49; Lam 1:12; Jn 16:22

My Jesus, grant me a tender love for You and Your holy Mother.

5. JESUS IS HELPED BY SIMON
Mt 25:40; Gal 6:2; Jn 13:16

Jesus, make me better understand the value of my sufferings which should

lead me closer to You, as Simon was
united with You through the Cross.

6. JESUS AND VERONICA

Is 52:14; Jn 14:9; Heb 1:3

Lord Jesus, increase the beauty of my
soul and fill me with joy and peace.
Jesus, give me courage.

7. JESUS FALLS A SECOND TIME

Ps 118:13; Heb 4:15; Mt 11:28

Jesus, I repent for having offended
You. Help me to avoid sin in the
future.

8. JESUS SPEAKS TO THE WOMEN

Lk 23:28; Jn 15:6; Lk 13:3

Merciful Jesus, make me weep for
my sins, which caused Your ter-
rible sufferings and the loss of my
friendship with You.

9. JESUS FALLS A THIRD TIME

Ps 22:15f; Phil 2:5-7; Lk 14:11

Jesus, grant that I may never yield to
despair in time of hardship and spiritu-

al distress. Let me come to You for help and comfort.

10. JESUS IS STRIPPED OF HIS GARMENTS
Ps 22:19; Lk 14:33; Rom 13:14

Grant, Lord Jesus, that I may sacrifice all my attachments rather than imperil the Divine life of my soul.

11. JESUS IS NAILED TO THE CROSS
Ps 22:17f; Lk 23:34; Jn 6:38

Jesus, strengthen my faith and increase my love for You. Help me to keep the Commandments.

12. JESUS DIES ON THE CROSS
Jn 12:32; Lk 23:46; Phil 2:8-9

Help me to forgive all those who have injured me, so that I myself may obtain forgiveness from You.

13. JESUS IS TAKEN FROM THE CROSS
Lk 24:26; Ps 119:165; 1 Jn 4:9f

Jesus, grant me through Your Mother's intercession to lead the life of a loyal child of Mary, so that I may be received into her arms at my death.

14. JESUS IS LAID IN THE SEPULCHER

Jn 12:24; Rom 6:10f; 1 Cor 15:4

Jesus, strengthen my good will to live for You until the Divine life of my soul will be manifested in the bliss of heaven.

Prayer before a Crucifix

O GOOD and gentle Jesus, look upon me here before You. With the most fervent desire of my soul I beg You to impress upon my heart lively sentiments of faith, hope, and charity. Grant me true repentance for my sins and a firm purpose of amendment.

With deep affection and grief of soul I ponder within myself and mentally contemplate Your five most precious wounds, having before my eyes what David spoke in prophecy about You, O good Jesus: "They have pierced My hands and feet; they have numbered all My bones."